GLACIERS
Nature's Frozen Rivers

GLACIERS
Nature's Frozen Rivers

Hershell H. Nixon and
Joan Lowery Nixon

Illustrated with photographs

DODD, MEAD & COMPANY • NEW YORK

Library of Congress Cataloging in Publication Data

Nixon, Hershell H.
    Glaciers, nature's frozen rivers.

    Includes index.
    SUMMARY: Discusses what glaciers are, how they move, the various kinds, how they move and change the land, and how they can be used.
    1. Glaciers—Juvenile literature. [1. Glaciers] I. Nixon, Joan Lowery, joint author. II. Title.
GB2403.8.N59   551.3'12   79-24655
ISBN 0-396-07802-8

For Gilbert and Whirlie Nixon

Acknowledgments

With gratitude to:
Dr. Mark F. Meier, Project Chief,
Dr. Steven Hodge,
Austin Post,
Donnie MacGowan,
and Ken Daniels
of the Glaciology Project Office,
United States Geological Survey,
for their kind assistance.

GLACIERS
Nature's Frozen Rivers

As the Margerie Glacier, in Glacier Bay, Alaska, moves forward, the chunks of ice that break off and crash into the sea are up to 200 feet (60 meters) high.

Down comes the snow, sometimes a drifting of tiny flakes, sometimes a swirling of flakes so thick that the sky is a sheet of blinding white. It is so cold that when the sky clears the snow does not melt. Year after year each heavy snow piles upon the one before it. As the temperature varies slightly, the snowflakes change into ice crystals.

Some of the surface snow melts, and the water seeps down into the mass of ice crystals, squeezing out a part of the trapped air. The weight of the layers of ice crystals squeezes out more air. The crystals are packed into a solid field of ice, which is known as an *ice field*.

The weight of the new snow on top adds to the weight of the ice. This mass grows heavier as it grows thicker. It presses downward with such force that this field of ice begins to move. Grinding and scraping the surface of the ground below, it slowly spreads outward. It rips boulders from the bedrock and drags them along. It carves its way through the mountain peaks. It moves outward and downward, flowing across the land.

It has become a glacier.

The huge sheet of ice that covers much of Greenland is a continental glacier.

WHAT IS A GLACIER?

A glacier is land ice that is moving because of the push of its great weight and the pull of gravity that draws it downward.

The shape of each glacier is different, because each surface over which ice flows will be different. And each glacier has its own mixture of dust, soil, and rock particles with its packed ice crystals.

Large glaciers which spread over entire mountains or plains are called *ice sheets*, or *icecaps*. Huge ice sheets which cover all or much of continents are called *continental glaciers*. These cover the North and the South poles and great parts of Greenland and Antarctica.

Valley glaciers are those rivers of ice that spread out from the ice fields, and follow existing mountain valleys. Some of the oldest glaciers may have carved their own valleys in the mountain rock. The smallest valley glaciers, like those in the Rocky Mountains, are just a few hundred yards long. Other glaciers, such as those in Alaska, are many miles long. The huge Beardmore Glacier in Antarctica is 300 miles long (482.7 kilometers) and 12 miles wide (19 kilometers)!

LaPerouse Glacier is an Alaskan tidewater glacier which flows into the Pacific Ocean. The base of the glacial snout is covered at high tide, exposed at low tide.

Tidewater glaciers are those which extend to the sea. As the ice meets the water, cliffs are formed. These cliffs are called the *snouts* of the glaciers. As the force of the ice presses downward toward the snout of a glacier, and water undermines the face of the cliff, large chunks of ice break off and fall into the water. When this happens it is said that the glacier is *calving*.

Glaciers which are melting, uncovering land or water which once was covered with ice, are called *retreating glaciers*.

This Alaskan glacier, which seems to hang high in a valley, is a retreating glacier.

While some glaciers have retreated over the years, many other glaciers have continued to grow, and new glaciers are being formed. Growing glaciers are constantly being fed by new snowfalls and by avalanches of large masses of snow that break off and sweep down the valley sides, piling up on the surface of the glacier.

As the glacier grows, it moves.

How Does a Glacier Move?

It is difficult to say exactly how long it takes to change snow into a glacier. Much would depend on the changes in temperature and how much it snows. It would be possible for a glacier to form within a period of a few years, and it would still be possible for the process to take a thousand years. When the mass of ice becomes thick enough, the glacier begins to move.

Different parts of a glacier move at different rates of speed, and many laws of nature are in action.

The bottom ice meets resistance as it rubs against the ground. The sides of a valley glacier meet with the same friction against the walls of the valley. The ice in the center of the glacier moves faster than that against the walls. *Gla-*

Helicopters are sometimes used for transportation in the study of glaciers.

ciologists (scientists who study glaciers) think that glaciers move because the ice crystals slowly change shape under the weight of the ice on top.

The glacier becomes a tongue of ice that moves downhill, faster at its center. Glaciologists have drilled holes in some glaciers and put in long, steel pipes. The movement of the ice near the bottom of the glacier has bent the pipes.

They have hammered stakes in a straight row across the

top of a glacier to measure its movement, and after a time the row of stakes has curved forward at the center.

Now United States Geological Survey glaciologists are measuring some fast-flowing glaciers with photography. Aerial photographs of a glacier have been taken every two months from close to the same position. When these photographs are compared, the movement of the glacier is noted.

Some glaciers react to weather changes more quickly than others. Glaciologists have found that changes in the weather cause rapid changes in Coleman and Roosevelt glaciers on the steep sides of Mount Baker, Washington.

Through these photographs, the glaciologists can determine changes in the thickness of the ice and the rate of glacier flow.

The rate of movement in a glacier is not always the same. It moves faster in the summer and slower in the winter. The thicker the glaciers are, and the steeper the slopes on which they lie, the faster they move. Glaciologists know that the presence of water at the bed, or bottom, of the glacier, and the pressure of this water, affects the sliding of the glacier. They are studying the causes of changes in rates of movement.

Dr. Steven Hodge, at the United States Geological Survey Glaciology Project Office in Tacoma, Washington, is making tests at the South Cascade Glacier in Washington, where the main research station is located. He is drilling into the glacier to connect with the flow of water under the glacier. There he measures the water pressure. The South Cascade Glacier is not a fast-moving glacier. It moves only about a yard, or a meter, a month.

The world's fastest flowing glacier is the Jacobshavns Glacier in Greenland. It moves between 160 and 200 feet (48 to 60 meters) a day.

The Malaspina Glacier in Alaska is changed from a valley glacier into a piedmont glacier as it spreads out onto the open, flat countryside. The dark swirls are stripes of lateral moraine which has been carried down from the mountains.

Some glaciers move in sudden surges. They build up a reservoir of snow and ice which suddenly slides downhill. Then they have a period of quiet in which the snow and ice build up again, until they are once more released like a flood. No one knows why this happens.

Sometimes glaciers spill from valleys out into open country. There the glaciers spread out into flat, wide sheets of ice, still moving forward.

They are called *piedmont glaciers* if they come from valley glaciers. They are called *outlet glaciers* if they spill from ice sheets.

This icefall from the Greenland ice sheet looks like a frozen waterfall. It spreads into an outlet glacier.

Where Can Glaciers Be Found in the United States?

Among other things, the state of Alaska is famous for its many glaciers. At least 3 percent of the state (about 17,000 square miles, or 44,030 square kilometers) is covered by glaciers.

In the continental United States, Washington State has an estimated 800 glaciers, which cover about 160 square miles (414 square kilometers). Glaciers are found in Wyoming, Montana, Oregon, California, Colorado, Idaho, Nevada, and Utah. Many of these are small glaciers, just big enough to be counted.

Crevasses

There are two kinds of ice in a glacier, and they behave differently. The ice in the lower part of the glacier has so much pressure on it that it "flows" over the ground beneath it. Any water at the bed of the glacier helps it move.

But the top layer of ice—100 to 200 feet thick (30.48 to 60.96 meters)—is brittle and breaks easily. When one part of a glacier moves faster than another part, this top ice can't adjust to the change, and it cracks, causing loud noises like firecrackers.

Hikers study a deep crevasse in the King's Glacier on West Spitsbergen Island, Norway.

The cracks that are found in the ice are called *crevasses*. They can be very deep and wide and dangerous, or very shallow. Crevasses often appear where the glacier passes over a rise in the valley floor, or where the slope of the valley increases. This gives glaciologists clues as to what the ground surface might be like under the ice.

Some crevasses form along the sides of glaciers, where the slower-moving ice can't keep up with the faster-moving ice at the center.

These crevasses have shown glaciologists that a glacier is made up of layers of dirty and clean ice. The winter snows are the clean ice. The summer warmth brings melted snows from the sides of the valleys. These snows carry rock and dirt. Layers of dust settle on top of the snow. When winter comes again the dirt, rock, and dust are frozen into the layer of ice. Then new snows cover them and become a layer of clean ice.

At times a stream of melted ice from a glacier carries rocks with it and runs into a crevasse. The rocks are often swirled around at the bottom of the crevasse, carving out a cave in the ice. Sometimes the stream disappears into the ice. Sometimes it joins other streams and continues under the glacier, cutting a tunnel to the foot of the glacier and forming other caves in the ice. Occasionally these caves

This ice cave was caused by water flowing at the base of the glacier.

A glacial stream has cut an ice tunnel at the base of the Matanuska Glacier in Alaska.

are open and large enough to be explored, such as the caves in Paradise Glacier on Mount Rainier in Washington.

Measuring the Ice

When ice is at freezing temperature it is called *temperate ice*. The ice in most valley glaciers is temperate ice. When ice is below freezing it is called *polar ice*. Polar ice has no liquid water in it. Temperate ice has.

For many years glaciologists have taken cores of polar

ice by drilling deeply into the ice and bringing up long, round sections of the ice. These cores show the layers of ice. Some layers show heavy snowfall. Some show volcanic ash and other pollutants, such as sulfur dioxide, lead, and radioactive materials, which were carried through the air to mix with the snow layers.

Volcanic ash gives glaciologists a good way of finding time periods in a core. They can match the layer of frozen ash to the date of a large volcanic eruption. Then they can date the layers above and below it.

They can test the pollutants in the ice layers and dis-

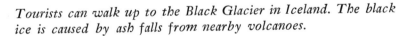

Tourists can walk up to the Black Glacier in Iceland. The black ice is caused by ash falls from nearby volcanoes.

cover what these chemicals are. Sometimes they can tell how far the pollutants have traveled, when they know these chemicals are used only in certain countries.

A new way to measure the thickness of temperate ice and polar ice is by *monopulse radar*. Two antennas are put on the ice, and a radar wave is sent into the ice from one antenna. The wave bounces from the ground below the ice and goes to the other antenna. The travel time is measured. Knowing the speed, the thickness of the ice can then be calculated.

This method of measuring the depth of ice has been used on ice up to about 3,000 feet (914 meters) thick. Attempts are now being made to take radar readings which measure the thickness of the ice from aircraft flying above the ice.

ICEBERGS

When tidewater glaciers meet the sea and calve, these chunks of ice are called *icebergs*. Not all icebergs come from glaciers. Some are chunks of ice that break away from ice packs made by frozen seawater. But the icebergs that do come from glaciers are many and are found in all sizes.

Only 80 feet (24 meters) of this huge iceberg show above the water. Below the surface the ice extends 560 feet (170 meters)!

Some of them are as large as big buildings. Some icebergs are so large that as they move they scrape the ocean floor, digging furrows. Engineers who lay cables across the ocean floor have learned not to put them in the places where these icebergs travel.

Large icebergs are a danger to ships, because most of the ice is hidden under the water where it can't be seen. If a ship should run into this hidden ice, it could be ripped open.

This happened to a passenger ship, the *Titanic*, on April 14, 1912, just before midnight, when it hit the hidden ice of an iceberg in the Atlantic Ocean. Less than one-third of

Normally the Ice Patrol is carried out by United States Coast Guard planes. Only when there is a large number of icebergs threatening shipping lanes are cutters like this one called out for standby to warn ships.

the 1,500 passengers and crew members of the *Titanic* were saved.

Because of this disaster the International Ice Patrol was formed, with the United States Coast Guard taking an active part. Icebergs breaking from the ice sheets of Antarctica and Greenland float for thousands of miles before melting in the warmer gulf stream waters, and they cross many shipping lanes. Pilots of Coast Guard planes are able to spot these icebergs and warn ships to avoid them.

How Glaciers Change the Land

When a glacier moves it marks and changes the ground beneath it. As large boulders are pulled from their bedrock and pushed along with the river of ice, the immense weight above them causes them to cut grooves and scratches (*striations*) in the bedrock below. Glaciers have carved out some of our mountains' most beautiful peaks and valleys.

Valleys which have been cut by rivers are V-shaped. But valleys which have been carved out by glaciers, with their grinding rocks and ice, are rounded out at the bottom, like a U.

Hanging valleys are often found leading into glacial valleys. These U-shaped valleys are called "hanging valleys" because they have a higher valley floor than the central glacial valleys. The glaciers that created these hanging valleys were smaller and did not cut as deeply into the bedrock as did the main glaciers, which they joined. Glaciers still exist in some hanging valleys.

Often a waterfall drops from the edge of a hanging valley into the glacial valley below. Yosemite Falls is an example. The Upper and Lower falls combined drop 2,425 feet (739 meters), making it one of the highest waterfalls in the world.

Cirques are bowl-shaped hollows carved into the rocks by beginning glaciers. As a glacier forms, the ice plucks

The bridal falls of Yosemite National Park drop from a hanging glacial valley into a larger glacial valley. Both valleys have a wide U shape.

West Carter Glacier in Glacier National Park, Montana, continues to carve a cirque more deeply.

Glaciers carved many cirques and left jagged horns on the famous Matterhorn mountain in Switzerland.

boulders from the sides and the bottom of an already existing low place, making it deeper. Over the years, as this process goes on, the walls of the cirques become jagged and steep. Some of these rough peaks, where a number of cirques have been formed close together, are called *horns*, such as the Matterhorn in Switzerland. In the Grand Teton mountains in Wyoming there are many of these jagged peaks caused by cirques, such as Mount Moran.

Some cirques contain beginning glaciers; many are now empty; a few contain patches of ice and snow; and some hold lakes from melted glaciers. These cirque lakes are called *tarns*.

Long ago some glaciers carved deeply into the rock on their way to the sea. After they melted, the sea came in to fill their valleys. These valleys, called *fjords*, have walls that are steep and high, and their water is deep. The Sogne Fjord in Norway, for example, is 120 miles long (193 kilometers). This fjord has cliffs that are as high as 3,000 feet (914 meters), and water that is 4,000 feet deep (1,219 meters) in places.

Fjords are found in many of the northern countries, and

Deep within this cirque, icebergs float in a lake from the melted glacier which carved the rock. (Glacier National Park).

Norway is a land of many beautiful fjords. These deep, sea-filled valleys were carved by glaciers of the ice ages.

in Chile and New Zealand, where glaciers once extended from the Antarctic ice fields. Some are tourist attractions, because of their rugged beauty; many are large and deep enough to be used by passenger ships and freighters.

As glaciers moved down valleys, they sometimes traveled over beds of rock that did not move. As the ice slid over and around them it wore the rock to gentle, smooth, rounded humps. The rocks were deeply gouged in the direction in which the glacier was moving, and the surfaces of the rocks were smoothly polished by the sandpaper effect of the sand and gravel sliding over them. When these rocks are found in clusters, they often have the shape of

The grooves in the rock from lower left to upper right show that the glacier that carved them moved in that direction. In the background, among the trees, are rounded sheepback rocks.

These boulders of different sizes were carried away from their original locations by glaciers. They are called glacial erratics.

grazing sheep; so they are called *sheepback rocks*, or *sheep rocks*. These rocks show scientists the direction in which the glacier ice was moving.

Other rocks were plucked from their own bedrock and were carried by glaciers for many miles. They are different from the bedrock in the areas in which they are found, so they are called *glacial erratics*. They vary in size from huge boulders to small pebbles. As an example, near Kotzebue, above the Arctic Circle in western Alaska, are found large boulders of green jade, which were left there by ancient glaciers. No one knows the source of the jade. It is known only that the boulders are not native to the area in which they are found.

Moraines

Glaciers pick up and carry great amounts of rock, sand, clay, dust, and particles ground so fine that they are called *glacial flour*. All of this material is known as *glacial drift*. There are two kinds of drift. *Till* is a mixture of unlayered pieces of rock, ranging in size from huge boulders to clay.

Glacial meltwater usually carries a milky glacial flour. When a clear, spring-fed stream joins the glacial stream, the contrast can be seen.

Terminal moraine dammed a meltwater stream from Mystery Glacier in the Olympic Mountains in Washington, creating this lake.

It has been carried and left by the ice from glaciers. *Outwash* is drift that has been left in definite layers by the water from melting glaciers.

Many of the land forms made up of till are called *moraines*, which means "broken stones." In some glaciers it is easy to see the stripes of till that are carried downstream by the glaciers. The till which is deposited at the foot of a glacier, where the ice melts, is called *terminal moraine*.

Glaciologists can tell if a glacier melted quickly or slowly by the size of its terminal moraine. If the pile of rocks is high, then the glacier had been there for a long time, adding soil and rocks over the years. If the ridge of rocks is not very high, then it shows that the glacier melted fairly quickly.

Lateral moraines are ridges of stones left along the sides of a melted glacier.

Ground moraines are the sediments that were spread over the land by the huge ice sheets that once covered large

These twisted stripes of lateral moraine show there were periods of surges in the Susitana Glacier, which is in the area of Mount McKinley in Alaska.

portions of the earth. Much of the fertile soil in our Midwest and northern states was created in this way.

In areas in which there is a layer of ground moraine, groups—or fields—of smooth, oval-shaped hills can be found. These hills, called *drumlins*, have their narrower ends pointing in the direction the ice was moving. The sizes and shapes of drumlins vary. Many of them are less than half a mile long (500 meters), 25 to 100 feet high (7 to 30 meters), and 500 feet wide (150 meters). Many drumlin fields are found in Canada, Michigan, Wisconsin, New York, Minnesota, and Massachusetts. Part of the city of Boston is built on a drumlin field.

The drumlins in this field in Saskatchewan, Canada, show the direction taken by glaciers of long ago.

This glacial deposit, in the form of a serpentine esker, is found in the state of Michigan.

Long, low, winding hills, which can be many miles in length, are made up of till and are called *eskers*. The name came from Ireland, where it means "path" or "ridge." Eskers show the path of long-ago, slow-moving bodies of ice.

Other mounds left by glaciers are *kames*, which scientists think were made from sand and gravel that washed into holes in glaciers. When the glaciers melted, they left these small hills, shaped like cones.

Near kames are often found holes called *kettles*. These holes were formed when large chunks of ice melted, and the sides of the drift around the ice caved in. Some of these kettles are filled with water and have formed lakes. These kettle lakes measure from just a few feet across to nearly a mile in diameter.

Sometimes the drift that was left by a glacier of long ago was large enough to plug a glacial valley, and a lake was formed. Many of the long, narrow lakes in our northern states were formed by glaciers. These lakes run in a general

Right: A lake fills this kettle near Mendenhall Glacier, Alaska. The kettle was formed by the melting of a large chunk of ice. Below: Glaciers of the ice ages left cone-shaped kames. These kames are south of Columbus, Ohio.

north-south direction, following the pattern of the movement of the great ice sheets.

In this same way old riverbeds have been blocked, and rivers have had to make new beds. The Columbia River flows in a valley which it created after its way in the old, Grand Coulee bed was blocked by an icecap.

Meltwater from glacial ice formed many very large lakes, such as Lake Bonneville in Utah, which reached into Nevada and Idaho. The old shoreline for this once giant lake can be found along the sides of nearby mountains. What is left of Lake Bonneville is called the Great Salt Lake.

THE ICE AGES

Scientists can tell, from fossils and rock layers, that two or three million years ago much of the earth that is now cold was tropical and hot. The weather changed, and a gradual cooling began. At the poles it began to snow. Scientists can guess that it snowed for many hundreds of years, and this snow packed itself into huge ice fields. The immense weight caused the ice fields to move; and the glaciers from the north spread down to cover Canada and some of

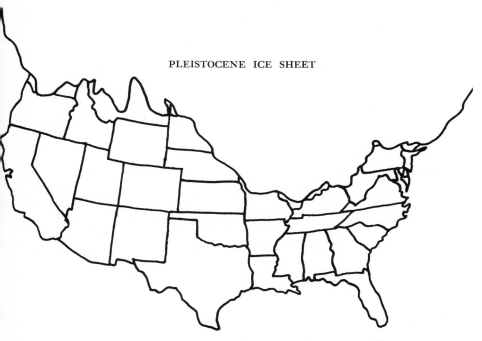

During the great ice ages, which began about one million years ago, continental ice sheets covered much of Canada and the northern United States.

the United States, moving in a large fan shape over the mid-northern states as far as St. Louis, Missouri. The Rocky Mountains and coastal mountains were covered by glaciers.

Glaciers spread down into Europe and Russia, and the ice at the South Pole spread upward into Africa, New Zealand, Australia, and the lower South American countries. Scientists think that at least one-third of the surface of the earth at one time was covered by ice.

There were four ice ages that are known. Through these ages there were warming periods and cooling periods. It is not known why these changes took place.

Learning about the ice ages and glaciers came slowly and in stages, with one idea building upon another. In the early eighteen hundreds Charles Lyell in Scotland decided that the earth had changed very gradually, and that rocks and boulders that were out of place probably had been carried there from the Arctic by huge cakes of ice (icebergs) and left when the ice melted. He called this material "drift," because he felt it had drifted down on the cakes of ice.

A number of years later a group of Swiss scientists came up with another theory. They saw that the glaciers in the Swiss Alps moved downhill carrying drift. It made more sense to them that glaciers would carry this material instead of ice cakes, because where would floating ice cakes pick up loose rocks and soil? They thought there must have been a great spread of ice over the earth long before men lived on earth.

A Swiss engineer, J. Venetz-Sitten, found drift left by glaciers in many places in England and Germany. He also found rocks that had been deeply scratched, and he realized that glaciers had caused these grooves and scratches. In 1821, he said he believed a giant glacier had flowed north out of Switzerland to cover these parts of the earth.

In 1834, a zoologist named Louis Agassiz, reported that he did not think there had been enough ice in the Alps to cause the former ice fields. He thought the ice had come

Glacial striations in this boulder at Mendenhall Glacier, Alaska, run from left to right. The white line crossing them at an angle is a vein of calcite.

from the far north. Charles Lyell added that many rocks he studied showed the direction of glacial scratches did not come from the North Pole, but from Sweden and Norway!

Soon afterward, scientists in the United States began to realize that the North American continent probably had been covered with a larger ice sheet than that which had spread over parts of Europe.

In the years since the ice ages were discovered, and glaciologists in the United States began to study the ancient glaciers on this continent, they have divided the times of the intense cold on the North American continent into four periods: Nebraskan, the oldest, followed by Kansan, Illinoin, and Wisconsin. The names mark the distances the ice reached. In different parts of Europe different names for the four ice ages are used.

The warmer periods in between the ice ages are named in the United States: Aftonia, the oldest, followed by Yarmouth and Sangamon. These are also Midwest names.

Glaciologists have mapped the areas which were covered by ice, and have shown that the coastal areas of the United States were changed. During the times of the large ice sheets, the sea level was lowered about 450 feet (137 meters) from the present level, as some of the frozen water came from the oceans.

WILL THERE BE ANOTHER ICE AGE?

Some *climatologists* (scientists who study the long range climate of the world) think that we are living in a period with a warming trend. Some feel that by adding pollution to the air and cutting down forests, and building larger cities which substitute cement for grasslands, we are changing earth's natural balancers. This could cause further warming, and even a future heat wave.

Others point out that these same facts could mean a future cooling of the earth. They note that our winters have grown longer, with the average worldwide temperatures dropping half a degree Fahrenheit. And they observe that the ice which covers the arctic regions of the northern hemisphere has been steadily and slowly increasing.

Will there be another ice age? There could be, but not in our lifetimes. The changes from warmer periods to colder periods cover so many thousands of years that no

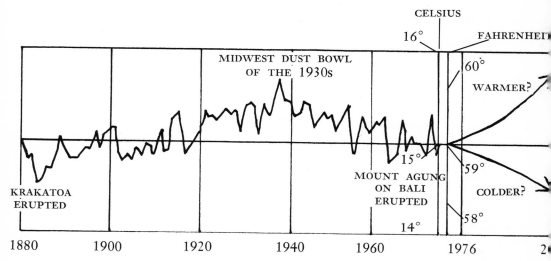

A history of weather in the Northern Hemisphere. When volcanoes Krakatoa and Mount Agung erupted, their dust circled the earth and cooled the global climate. Since 1938 there has been a downward trend of temperature.

one could actually feel the changes in temperature taking place. Climatologists who think there will be another ice age believe that it will not begin to build up for another 10,000 to 100,000 years!

How Can We Use Glaciers?

The glaciers of the ice ages left many benefits: the fertile fields of rich soil, the finely ground gravel deposits, the many lakes as sources of water, and majestic mountain scenery.

And we have uses for the glaciers in existence today. The water supply for some cities comes from nearby glaciers. The people of Tacoma, Washington, use the stream-flow from the Nisqually Glacier for hydroelectric power. The citizens of Boulder, Colorado, enjoy the water supply from Arapaho Glacier, which they own. In 1919, Congress passed a bill allowing the city of Boulder to buy from the government the land containing the glacier.

About 15 percent of the summer flow of the Columbia River comes from glaciers in Canada, and hydroelectric power and irrigation water in some northwest communities comes from melting glacier water. The United States Geological Survey has reported that over three-fourths of all the fresh water in the world is frozen into glacier ice.

Glaciers are the best natural reservoir for water, providing water when it is needed the most. Rain-fed rivers have their peak flow during rainy seasons when water isn't needed as much; but glacier-fed rivers reach their peak during hot, summer weather, when the need for water is great.

Glaciologists build a station to measure the amount of meltwater from a glacier.

During a severe drought in Chile the rain-fed rivers dried up; but some of the glacier ice melted in the heat, and the glacier-fed rivers brought much needed water to the people.

Some people hope it will be possible in the future to take

A massive icefall from the Tahoma Glacier on Mount Rainier, Washington.

glacier ice to countries which need water. First steps are being taken to attempt to tow large icebergs to dry countries, to increase their water supply. A prince in Saudi Arabia has formed a company called Iceberg Transport International. He has predicted that by the year 2000, Saudi Arabia will need more than 4 billion tons of water, and towing icebergs to the country would be less expensive than working out other ways of obtaining water.

Glaciers are not just remnants of ice ages past. They are growing, moving forces on the earth today. They are aiding scientists in their search to unlock some of the secrets of the past, and they are a natural resource to develop in our world of tomorrow.

Index

ABOUT THE AUTHORS

HERSHELL H. NIXON, a graduate of the University of Southern California, is a geologist for Strata Energy, Inc., in Houston, Texas, and a member of the American Association of Petroleum Geologists, the American Professional Geological Scientists, and the Houston Geological Society. This is the third book he has written with his wife, Joan.

JOAN LOWERY NIXON, also a graduate of the University of Southern California, has written many books for children—everything from picture books to young adult fiction. She is a member of the Board of Directors of the Society of Children's Book Writers. One of her books has won an Edgar scroll from the Mystery Writers of America, and one was winner of the Texas Institute of Letters best children's book award.

The authors' previous book in this series, *Volcanoes: Nature's Fireworks*, was selected as an Outstanding Science Trade Book for Children in 1978 by the National Science Teachers Association and the Children's Book Council Joint Committee.